VIEWS OF SURREY CHURCHES

VIEWS OF ALL THE CHURCHES AND CHAPELRIES IN THE COUNTY OF SURREY

by

CHARLES THOMAS CRACKLOW
Architect and Surveyor

Published by Phillimore & Co. Ltd.,
for the Surrey Local History Council
as Extra Volume No. 2 of Surrey History

1979

Published by
PHILLIMORE & CO. LTD.
London and Chichester

Head Office: Shopwyke Hall,
Chichester, Sussex, England

ISBN 0 85033 361 X

Printed in Great Britain by
GRAPHIC COLOUR PRINT
Emsworth · Hampshire

THE ARRANGEMENT OF PLATES IN
THE ORIGINAL WORK

INTRODUCTION

In his prospectus for this work, C. T. Cracklow stated his intentions 'to assist the Antiquary in his researches in Topography, the studious in the pursuit of general knowledge; and the Clergy in ascertaining the nature of their local rights; and the work will prove, also, an *ornamental* accompaniment to "Manning and Bray's History" as well as an useful appendage to other historical accounts of the County'. In his preface, dated June 1823, he says: 'The Author, having perused with attention and much satisfaction the "HISTORY OF SURREY, by MANNING AND BRAY," was anxious to transmit to posterity a correct relation of the present condition of the CHURCHES in that County. This object in the history just adverted to, has been but partially attained; owing to the immense expense and time which the execution of the necessary engravings would have required. The author, however, has been induced to undertake the present arduous task (connected, as it in some measure was, with his professional pursuits) of giving to the world such an account, accompanied with accurate delineations; by the facilities which the lately discovered art of Lithography afforded him, for an enterprise of this extensive nature.' The book has been virtually unobtainable for some twenty years and it is interesting to note that this reprint, sponsored by the Surrey Local History Council, to assist the members of their member societies in their researches, is only possible by another recent development in lithography, using metal plates, photographically produced.

Not a lot is known about Cracklow himself. He was a surveyor in Southwark and in 1796 was author of a scheme for the improvement of the Port of London. The topographical artist John Buckler is reputed to have been apprenticed to him.[1] Although in the preface and on most of the plates they are stated to be published from 1, Crane Court, Fleet Street, the last plate to be issued, that of Titsey Church, gives his address as 3, St. Bride's Court, Bridge Street, Blackfriars.

The work was issued in parts, each of six plates, at a cost of 7s. 6d. (6s. to subscribers). The plates were printed on one side of thin paper of Royal Quarto size, the majority being seven and a half inches square. All of the views are exteriors and are accompanied on each plate by a block plan and these are all to a common scale on the original of 64ft. to the inch. For this reprint they have been reduced in size, all by the same factor, but dimensions may still be taken from the scales provided. All were printed by lithography, a process which had been invented in Bavaria in 1798 and was first used in England in 1803.[2] The printer was P. Simonau or Simonau and Co., except for the plate of Titsey Church, by A. Fourquemin. Peter Simonau was at 43, Essex Street, Strand in 1822 and 24, Maiden Lane in 1826, but is believed to have moved to Brussels in 1828.[3] He may well have come from there, since several of the early lithographic printers came from the continent. The draughtsmanship appears to be in several hands, 54 (mainly those issued first) are signed by Charles Burton, 15 are by G. C-S. and four by W. F. S.; the rest are anonymous. Two attempts were made at the drawing of Bagshot Chapel and both have been reproduced. Apparently, the plans were by Cracklow himself. Each plate was accompanied by a page of letterpress text, set in an italic type. This relates more to the parish than the structure of the church and gives such information as the names of the incumbent and patron, whether the benefice is a rectory, vicarage or chapelry, the population from the census returns and some details of the endowments in some cases, thus fulfilling the author's third object, quoted above. Since this information is readily available in a more accurate form, the text has not been reprinted.[4]

The plates were published in paper covers in 26 parts. A slip with the first part, dated July 1823, apologises for the delay and promises regular publication of one or more numbers monthly until the work is completed. Three parts were finished by October 1823 and part 7 is dated 1824 on a new printed cover used for all subsequent parts. All of the part numbers are inserted by hand and the final parts 25 and 26 were issued together, but without text. From the dates Cracklow gives for the consecration of new churches it is clear that part 14 appeared after June 1824, part 15 after December 1824, part 22 after February 1825 and part 23 after July 1825. The date of the final part is uncertain but has been given as late as 1827.[5] One senses financial and production problems, a promised addendum and list of subscribers apparently never appearing. In October 1823 a circular concludes with 'on which account the applications of distant Subscribers with prompt payment will oblige'. Local history publication has never been very lucrative. The parts were available from the author and publisher at his office, at 'the Principal Booksellers and Stationers in every market town in the County' and from two London booksellers.

Cracklow studied the churches of the ancient county of Surrey, including parishes as far as Rotherhithe in the area taken for the London County Council. He attempted to illustrate all consecrated churches, even the 'Waterloo' Churches, the four new churches in Lambeth parish, and these must have been barely completed.[6] He included chapels of ease, whether ancient like Oakwood or Ripley or modern, provided they were consecrated, but did not include St. Catherine's, then as now a ruin, or Wanborough, then a barn. An exception was made for Stockwell chapel, although unconsecrated, because of 'the distinguished character of its trustees', but Dulwich College chapel, although consecrated, was mentioned but not illustrated. They were not the earliest such collection to be made, just the first to be published. The Sharpe Collection of 166 water colour drawings by Henry Petrie between 1790 and 1808 has recently been dispersed, but sets of photographs exist in the Minet Library and that of the Surrey Archaeological Society at Castle Arch.[7] John and Edward Hassell in the first half of the 19th century produced over 1700 views in Surrey including many church interiors and exteriors,[8] but the majority unfortunately remain unpublished.

These Cracklow views are of great value to the local historian and, although they may be somewhat sketchy, they appear in the cases which can be checked to be accurate and reliable. Their great merit is that they show many churches before the drastic 'restoration' which many were subsequently to receive. In this they are supplemented by Sir Stephen Glynne's contemporary notes on some 81 Surrey churches[9] and those of Arthur Hussey, published in 1852.[10] Some medieval churches had already been rebuilt; for example, Holy Trinity, Guildford (1763), Chertsey (1808), Egham (1820), Mitcham (1821) and several in South London. Some had been rebuilt and have since been swept away, as at Shalford (1790), Long Ditton (by no less an architect than Sir Robert Taylor, 1776) and the ornate gothic tower at Walton-on-the-Hill (1818). Some only remain as fragments, like the tower at Ewell or the chancel at Cheam and it is interesting to see what the rest of the church was like. It is often said how poor the churches of Surrey were, and while this might be true compared with those of the stone belt or of East Anglia, this collection shows us how varied they were and how much we have lost. Very few churches, in fact, remain unaltered and some have been completely rebuilt, but even in the limited space of this introduction a few features may be noted. The round tower at Tooting is shown and this was probably Norman.[11] There are three in Sussex in addition to a large group in Norfolk and Suffolk. Timber towers which have vanished are shown at Horne and Leigh, while the 13th-century example at Tandridge has been considerably altered. One of the greatest losses archaeologically in the County was the timber-framed church of 1606 at Frimley. Items of his father's or grandfather's generation are often most in danger from the zealous rebuilder and in this category fall the portico on the north side of Kingston Church, the tower at Effingham and the cupolas at Oxted and Farnham. The early 18th-century windows at Ash and the two tiers of windows to light aisles and galleries may be seen at Epsom and Godalming. Outside the church, a large number of the plates show wooden 'bedhead' monuments. The paved path at Charlwood was there in Cracklow's time and there was a combined lych-gate and stocks at Chobham. There was also a windmill near the new church of St. George, Camberwell and the bridge over the canal is in the foreground. The horizontal windmill can just be seen behind Battersea Church.

For further study of churches, the reader is referred to the works of Nairn and Pevsner[12] (who often give the name of the architect who rebuilt the church), the small handbook of Morris,[13] the careful analysis of Brown,[14] the sketches of P. M. Johnston,[15] and the several papers in *Surrey Archaeological Collections*. A good introduction to the subject was given recently by Blatch.[16]

I hope I may be permitted a personal reminiscence. I joined the Surrey Archaeological Society in 1944 as a schoolboy, when members who attended the excursions (under the very able organisation of Mr. J. Wilson-Haffenden) were keen ecclesiologists and many would carry notebooks to sketch the mouldings in the churches visited, as antiquarians had done for over two centuries. After the war, the discoveries in the bomb damage and the influence of television ensured that all young archaeologists were more interested in excavation and I now wish that I could have learned more from that older generation about churches, before so much of their practical expertise virtually died out. I sense an increasing interest in our churches and hope that this volume might help in this revival.

Chairman, Surrey Local History Council
September 1979
                                        KENNETH GRAVETT

NOTE: In this reprint, the plates have been reduced to give greater intensity, but even so on some occasions the captions and plans are not very clear due to the quality of the original.

REFERENCES

1. H. Colvin, *A Biographical Dictionary of British Architects 1600-1840* (1978), 237.
2. *Printing and the Mind of Man* (1960), 109.
3. M. Twyman, 'Directory of London Lithographic Printers', *J. Printing Historical Society* 10 (1974), 47.
   I thank Mr. G. Brydson, Librarian of the Linnaean Society, for this reference.
4. e.g. in *Victoria County History (V.C.H.)* (1902-1914).
5. Colvin, *op. cit.*
6. St. Luke, West Norwood was not consecrated until 15 July 1825; see K. R. Holdaway and M. D. Lambert, *St. Luke, West Norwood* (1974), 15.
7. *Surrey Archaeological Collections (Sy.A.C.)* 24 (1911), 176.
8. J. Batley, *A Picturesque Ride Through Surrey*; a catalogue of an exhibition at Guildford House, 1978.
9. R. J. Sherlock, 'Sir Stephen Glynne's Notes on the Churches of Surrey', *Sy.A.C.* 55 (1958), 65.
10. A. Hussey, *The Churches in the Counties of Kent, Sussex and Surrey, mentioned in the Domesday Book* (1852).
11. M. Keulemans, 'Old St. Nicholas's Church, Tooting Graveney', *Sy.A.C.* 57 (1960), 93.
12. I. Nairn, N. Pevsner and B. Cherry, *Buildings of England—Surrey* (1971); N. Pevsner, *Buildings of England—London II* (1952).
13. J. Morris, *County Churches—Surrey* (1910).
14. C. K. F. Brown, *Treasures of Surrey Churches in the Diocese of Guildford* (1943).
15. P. M. Johnston, 'Ecclesiastical Architecture', *V.C.H.* 2 (1905), 425.
16. M. Blatch, 'Surrey Churches—Saxon to Georgian', *Surrey History* 2 (1978), 4.

ABINGER CHURCH. N.E.

Ground Plan

Scale of 10   50   100 Feet

1. ABINGER

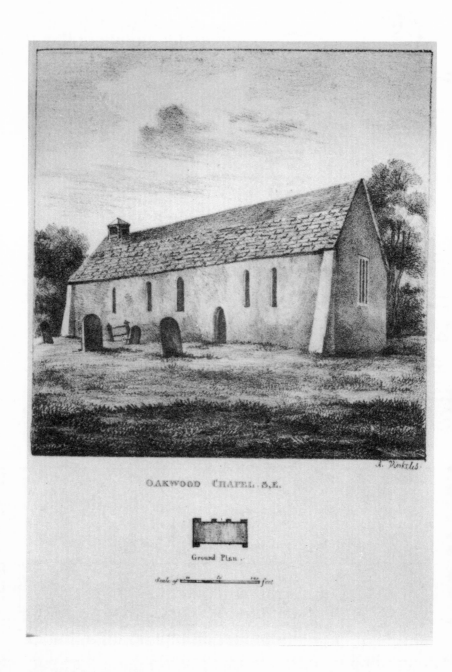

OAKWOOD CHAPEL. S.E.

Ground Plan.

Scale of [_____] feet

2. ABINGER, OAKWOOD CHAPEL

ADDINGTON CHURCH. S.E.

Ground Plan

Scale of ... 50 ... 100 Feet

3. ADDINGTON

ALBURY CHURCH, N.W.

Printed by P. Simoneau

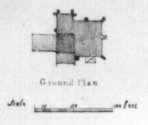

Ground Plan

Scale [10   20   100 Feet]

4. ALBURY

ALFOLD CHURCH &.E.

Printed by P.Simonau

Ground Plan

Scale of   Feet

5. ALFORD

ASH CHURCH. *S.E.*

Printed by Jonston

Ground Plan

Scale of _____ Feet

6. ASH

FRIMLEY CHURCH. S.

Ground Plan

7. ASH, FRIMLEY CHAPEL

ASHTEAD CHURCH &c.

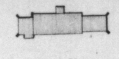

Ground Plan

Scale of 10   50   100 Feet

8. ASHTEAD

GC—s Printed by P.Simonau

BANSTEAD CHURCH. N.E.

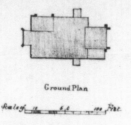

Ground Plan

Scale of ⟨...⟩ 100 Feet

9. BANSTEAD

C. Burln. del.   Printed by P. Simonau

BARNES CHURCH, South.

Ground Plan.

Scale of   .   .   .   .   .   feet

10. BARNES

BATTERSEA CHURCH, S.W.

Ground Plan.

11. BATTERSEA

C.Burton del.   Printed by P Simonau

BEDDINGTON CHURCH, S.W.

Ground Plan.

Scale of _____ 50 feet

12. BEDDINGTON

BERMONDSEY CHURCH, S.E.

Ground Plan

13. BERMONDSEY

BEACHWORTH CHURCH. *N.E.*

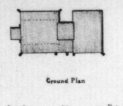

Ground Plan

Scale of ____ ____ ____ Feet

14. BETCHWORTH

BISLEY CHURCH, S.W.

Ground Plan

15. BISLEY

BLETCHINGLY CHURCH. S. W.

Ground Plan

Scale 0 ____ 50 ____ 100 Feet

16. BLECHINGLEY

BRAMLEY CHURCH, S.E.

Ground Plan.

Scale of   10   20   30 feet

17. BRAMLEY

C. Burton, delt.   Printed by P. Simonau

BUCKLAND CHURCH. S.E

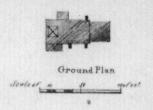

Ground Plan

Scale of 10   50   Feet 100

18. BUCKLAND

BURSTOW CHURCH. S.E.

Ground Plan

Scale of .... 50 .... Feet

19. BURSTOW

BYFLEET CHURCH. N.E

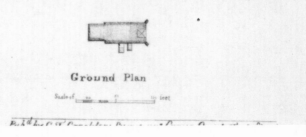

Ground Plan

Scale of 25 50 75 feet

20. BYFLEET

CAMBERWELL CHURCH N.W

Ground Plan

Scale of feet

21. CAMBERWELL

St GEORGE'S CHURCH, N.W. *CAMBERWELL*

Ground Plan

22. CAMBERWELL, ST. GEORGE

CAPEL CHURCH. S.E.

Ground Plan

23. CAPEL

C. Burton, delt   Printed by Simonau and Cᵒ

CARSHALTON CHURCH, N.W.

Ground Plan.

Scale of   10   40   90 feet

24. CARSHALTON

CATERHAM CHURCH, &c.

Ground Plan

25. CATERHAM

CHALDON, CHURCH. S.W.

Ground Plan

Scale of   Feet

26. CHALDON

Printed by Senneau

CHARLWOOD CHURCH *S E*

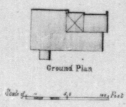

Ground Plan

Scale of   40   100 Feet

27. CHARLWOOD

Drawn by C.Burton.　　　　　　　　　　　　Printed by Simonav and

CHEAM CHURCH. S.E.

Ground Plan.

Scale of 0　　　50　　　90 feet

28.　CHEAM

CHELSHAM CHURCH S.E.

Ground Plan

29. CHELSHAM

CHERTSEY CHURCH.

Ground Plan

Scale of 2 — 5 — 10 Feet

30. CHERTSEY

CHESSINGTON CHURCH, S.W.

Ground Plan

Scale of   feet

31. CHESSINGTON

CHIDINGFOLD CHURCH &c.

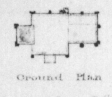

Ground Plan

32. CHIDDINGFOLD

CHIPSTED, CHURCH &c.

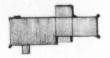

Ground Plan

Scale of _____ Feet

33. CHIPSTEAD

CHOBHAM CHURCH N.W

Printed by P.Simonau.

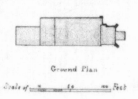

Ground Plan

Scale of _____ Feet

34. CHOBHAM

HOLY TRINITY CHURCH, NW CLAPHAM.

Ground Plan

35. CLAPHAM, HOLY TRINITY

SAINT PAUL'S CHAPEL, N.E. CLAPHAM

Ground Plan.

Scale of   60   feet

36. CLAPHAM, ST. PAUL

COBHAM CHURCH *N.E.*

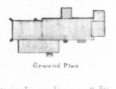

Ground Plan

37.   COBHAM

COMPTON CHURCH S.W.

Ground Plan

38. COMPTON

COULSDON. CHURCH. *South*.

Ground Plan.

Scale of |___10___|___60___|___200___| *Feet*

39. COULSDON

CRANLEY CHURCH, &c.

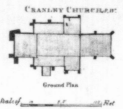

Ground Plan

Scale of _____ Feet

40. CRANLEIGH

CROWHURST CHURCH N-E

Ground Plan

Scale of 10 20 30 feet

41. CROWHURST

Chª Burton delᵗ   Printed by P. Simonau

CROYDON CHURCH, N.W.

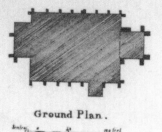

Ground Plan.

Scale: _____ 100 feet

42. CROYDON

DORKING CHURCH.

Ground Plan.

43. DORKING

C. Burton, delt.   Printed by ? Amours

DUNSFOLD CHURCH, S.

Ground Plan.

Scaled 0   10   w feet

44. DUNSFOLD

EAST CLANDON CHURCH &c.

Ground Plan

Scale of ... Feet

45. EAST CLANDON

EAST HORSLEY CHURCH &c.

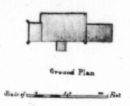

Ground Plan

Scale of ____ Feet

46. EAST HORSLEY

EAST MOULSEY CHURCH. N.W.

Printed by P.Simonau.

Ground Plan.

Scale of ... Feet

47. EAST MOLESEY

EFFINGHAM CHURCH. N.E.

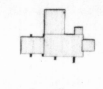

Ground Plan

Scale of   60   90 Feet

48. EFFINGHAM

EGHAM CHURCH N.º 17.

Ground Plan

Scale of   30   50   300 Feet

49. EGHAM

ELSTED CHURCH. N.E.

Printed by P. Simonau.

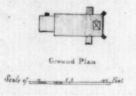

Ground Plan

Scale of

50. ELSTED

EPSOM CHURCH, N E

Ground Plan.

Scale of feet

51. EPSOM

ESHER CHURCH. N.W.

Ground Plan.

52. ESHER

C. Burton del.

Printed by P. Simonau

EWELL CHURCH. N.W.

Ground Plan.

53. EWELL

EWHURST CHURCH S.W.

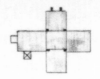

Ground Plan

Scale of   50   100 Feet

54. EWHURST

FARLEY CHURCH. S.E.

Ground Plan

Scale of

55. FARLEY

FARNHAM CHURCH, N.E.

Printed by P. Simonau

Ground Plan

Scale of   Feet.

56. FARNHAM

FETCHAM CHURCH. N.

Ground Plan

Scale 0   50   96 feet

57. FETCHAM

FRENSHAM CHURCH. S.W.

Printed by P.Simonau

Ground Plan.

Scale of .... Feet.

58. FRENSHAM

GATTON CHURCH. S.W.

Ground Plan

Scale of ___ ___ ___ Feet

59. GATTON

GODALMING CHURCH. S.W.

Ground Plan.

Scale of feet

60. GODALMING

GODSTONE CHURCH S.W

Ground Plan

61. GODSTONE

GREAT BOOKHAM CHURCH *S.W.*

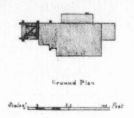

Ground Plan

Scale 0 50 100 Feet

62. GREAT BOOKHAM

HOLY TRINITY CHURCH, GUILDFORD. N.E.

Ground Plan.

63. GUILDFORD, HOLY TRINITY

ST MARY'S CHURCH N. GUILDFORD

Ground Plan

64. GUILDFORD, ST. MARY

Cha. Burton del.

Printed by P.Simonau

St. NICHOLAS CHURCH.W. *GUILDFORD.*

Ground Plan.

Scale of   50   feet

65. GUILDFORD, ST. NICHOLAS

HAMILTON CHURCH S.W.

Ground Plan

Scale of 25 50 100 Feet

66. HAMBLEDON

HASCOMBE CHURCH NOW.

Ground Plan

Scale of feet

67. HASCOMBE

HASLEMERE CHURCH.

Ground Plan.

Scale of ⌐————————————⌐ Feet.

68. HASLEMERE

HEADLEY CHURCH ≔E.

Ground Plan

Scale of 0   50   100 Feet

69. HEADLEY

HORLEY CHURCH &c.

Ground Plan

Scale of Feet

70. HORLEY

HORNE CHURCH&c.

Ground Plan

Scale of ——— ft ——— 100 Feet

71. HORNE

HORSHILL CHURCH, S-W

GroundPlan.

Scale of

72. HORSELL

KEW CHURCH. N.W.

Ground Plan

Scale of [   ] in Feet

73. KEW

C.Burton del.   Printed by P.Simonau

KINGSTON CHURCH. N·E

Ground Plan.

Scale of   10   50   100 feet

74. KINGSTON

LAMBETH CHURCH.

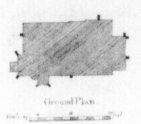

Ground Plan.

75.   LAMBETH, ST. MARY

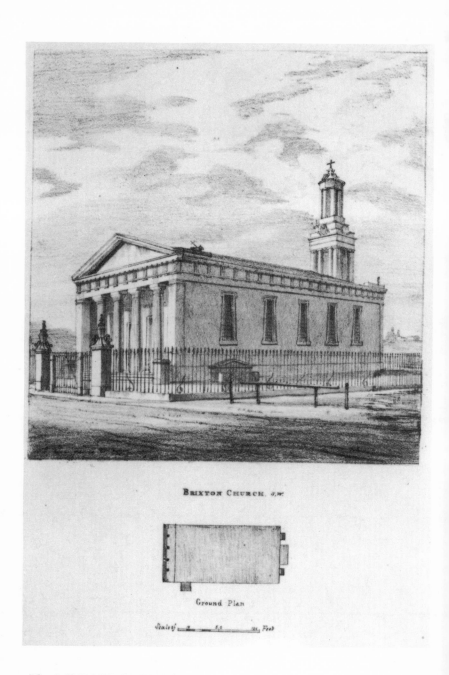

BRIXTON CHURCH. S.W.

Ground Plan

Scale of   0   50   100 Feet

76. LAMBETH, BRIXTON

KENNINGTON CHURCH.

Ground Plan

Scale of ___ ___ Feet

77. LAMBETH, KENNINGTON

NORWOOD CHURCH, *Lambeth*.

Ground Plan

Scale of ... ... Feet

78. LAMBETH, NORWOOD

WATERLOO CHURCH. SW

Ground Plan

79. LAMBETH, WATERLOO

STOCKWELL CHAPEL OF EASE to Lambeth Parish. S.W.

Ground Plan.

Scale of

80. LAMBETH, STOCKWELL CHAPEL

LEATHERHEAD CHURCH. N.E.

Printed by P.Simonau.

G.C. del

Ground Plan

Scale of ... Feet

81. LEATHERHEAD

LEIGH CHURCH SE

Ground Plan

Scale of

82. LEIGH

LIMPSFIELD CHURCH.W

Ground Plan.

83. LIMPSFIELD

LINGFIELD CHURCH. S.W

Ground Plan

84. LINGFIELD

LITTLE BOOKHAM CHURCH &c.

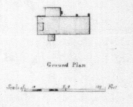

Ground Plan

Scale of 2 5.0 10 Feet

85. LITTLE BOOKHAM

LONG DITTON CHURCH. N.W.

Printed by C. Simonau.

Ground Plan

Scale of ____ 50 ____ 100 Feet

86. LONG DITTON

C Burton del.   Printed by P Simonau

MALDEN CHURCH. N.E.

Ground Plan.

87. MALDEN

MERROW CHURCH.

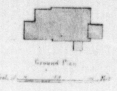

Ground Plan

88. MERROW

MERSTHAM CHURCH. S.W.

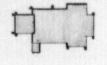

Ground Plan

Scale of 0 ___ 66 ___ 99 Feet

89. MERSTHAM

MERTON CHURCH. N·E.

Ground Plan.

Scale of

90. MERTON

MICKLEHAM CHURCH. N.W.

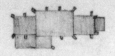

Ground Plan.

Published by C. T. Cracklow, Surveyor, Crane Court, Fleet Street.

91. MICKLEHAM

MITCHAM CHURCH.

Ground Plan.

92. MITCHAM

MORDEN CHURCH, S.E.

Ground Plan.

93. MORDEN

MORTLAKE CHURCH N.W.

C. Burton, del.t   Printed by P. Simonau

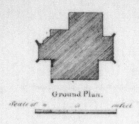

Ground Plan.

Scale of   feet

94. MORTLAKE

NEWDIGATE CHURCH, N.

Ground Plan.

95. NEWDIGATE

NEWINGTON CHURCH. S.W.

Ground Plan.

Scale [_____] feet

96. NEWINGTON

St. PETER'S CHURCH Newington.

Ground Plan

97.   NEWINGTON, ST. PETER

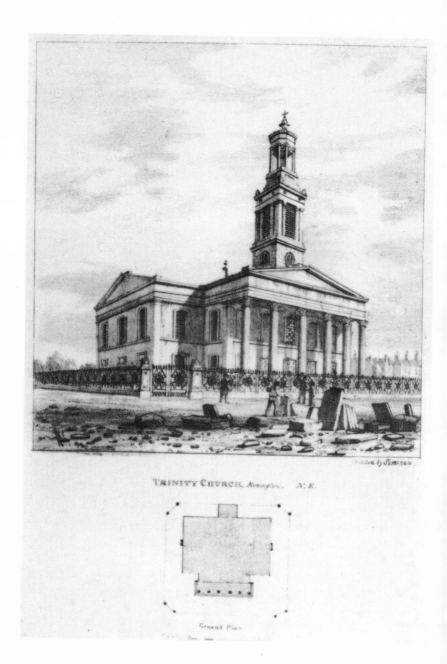

TRINITY CHURCH, *Newington.* *N. E.*

Ground Plan

98. NEWINGTON, TRINITY CHURCH

NUTFIELD CHURCH. N.E.

Ground Plan

99. NUTFIELD

OCKHAM CHURCH. *Nave*

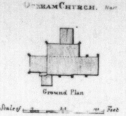

Ground Plan

Scale of ___ ___ Feet

100. OCKHAM

OCKLEY CHURCH. S.E.

Printed by Simson.

Ground Plan

Scale of [...] 50 [...] 100 Feet

101. OCKLEY

OXTED CHURCH N E

Ground Plan

Scale of feet

102. OXTED

G.C.   Printed by P.Simeau

PEPER-HAROW CHURCH, &E.

Ground Plan

Scale of ——————————— 100 Feet

103. PEPER HAROW

C. Burton del.   Printed by P Simonau

PETERSHAM CHURCH S W

Ground Plan

Scale of   feet

104. PETERSHAM

PIRBRIGHT *CHAPEL &c*, S.E.

Ground Plan

Scale

105. PIRBRIGHT

C Burton del.   Printed by P Simonau

PUTNEY CHURCH, S.W

Ground Plan.

106. PUTNEY

PUTTENHAM CHURCH *S.E.*

Printed by Blümenau.

Ground Plan

Scale of feet 50 100 Feet

107. PUTTENHAM

PIRFORD CHAPELRY, N E

Ground Plan.

Scale of 0 10 20 feet

108. PYRFORD

REIGATE CHURCH, S.E.

Ground Plan

Scale of [feet]

109. REIGATE

C.Burton del.?   Printed by P.Simonau

RICHMOND CHURCH. S.W.

Ground Plan

Scale of

110. RICHMOND

C.Burton, delt.

Printed by P Simonau

ROTHERHITHE CHURCH. S.W.

Ground Plan.

111. ROTHERHITHE

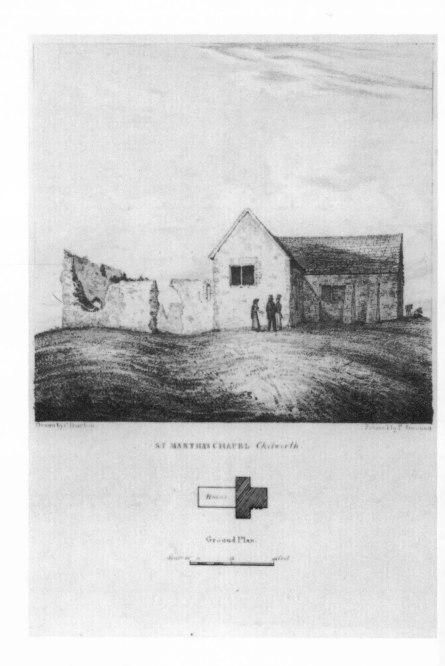

ST MARTHA'S CHAPEL *Chilworth*.

Ground Plan.

Scale to a 0 feet

112. ST. MARTHA

SANDERSTEAD CHURCH &c.

Ground Plan.

Scale of 0 50 100 Feet

113. SANDERSTEAD

SELE CHURCH. *S.W.*

Printed by P.Simonau.

Ground Plan

Scale of ___ ___ *Feet*

114. SEAL

SEND CHURCH N.W.

Ground Plan.

115. SEND

RIPLEY CHAPEL S E

Ground Plan

Scale of   10   100 Feet

116. SEND, RIPLEY CHAPEL

SHALFORD CHURCH. S.W.

Ground Plan

Scale of 10 , 5,0 , 100 Feet

117. SHALFORD

SHERE CHURCH. N.W

Ground Plan

Scale of 10   50   100 feet

Published by C. T. Cracklow, Surveyor, 4 Crane Court, Fleet Street.

118. SHERE

CHRIST CHURCH N.E

Ground Plan

119. SOUTHWARK, CHRISTCHURCH

St GEORGES CHURCH, S.W. SOUTHWARK.

Ground Plan.

120. SOUTHWARK, ST. GEORGE THE MARTYR

St JOHN'S CHURCH. N.W. *SOUTHW*

Printed by P. Simonau.

C. Burton del.

Ground Plan.

Scale

121. SOUTHWARK, ST. JOHN, HORSLEYDOWN

C.Burton del.

Printed by P.Simonau

St. OLAVE'S *SOUTHWARK SE.*

Ground Plan.

Scale of   0   50   100 feet

122. SOUTHWARK, ST. OLAVE

St SAVIOUR'S CHURCH; N.W. in *SOUTHWARK*.

Ground Plan

Scale of

123. SOUTHWARK, ST. SAVIOUR

C. Burton del.   Printed by P. Simonau

ST THOMAS'S CHURCH. S.E. *SOUTHWARK*

Ground Plan

Scale

124. SOUTHWARK, ST. THOMAS

STOKE D'ABERNON CHURCH NW

Printed by P.Simonau.

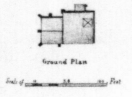

Ground Plan

Scale of   10   50   80 Feet

125. STOKE D'ABERNON

STOKE CHURCH next GUILDFORD, S.W.

Ground Plan.

Scale of 0   50   100 feet

126. STOKE NEXT GUILDFORD

C.Burton.del   Printed by P.Simonau

STREATHAM CHURCH.S.E

GroundPlan.

Scale of   m.feet

127. STREATHAM

SUTTON CHURCH, N.E.

Ground Plan

Scale of 0   50   100 feet

128. SUTTON

TANDRIDGE CHURCH, S.ST

GroundPlan

129. TANDRIDGE

TATTESFIELD CHURCH N. E.

Printed by P.Simonau

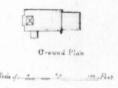

Ground Plan

Scale of

130. TATSFIELD

THAMES DITTON CHURCH. N.W.

Printed by P. Simonau.

Ground Plan

Scale of ... 50 ... 100 Feet

131. THAMES DITTON

THORP CHURCH. &c.

Ground Plan

Scale of 20 — 5 p 100 Feet

132. THORPE

THURSLEY CHURCH. S. E.

Ground Plan.

Scale of   Feet.

133. THURSLEY

TITSEY CHURCH,

Ground Plan

Scale of

Printed by J. Graf, Lincoln's Inn 33 Bride Court Bridge St Blackfriars.

134. TITSEY

TOOTING CHURCH .S-W.

C.Burton.delt.   Printed by P.Simonau

Ground Plan.

Scale of   10   40   100 feet

135. TOOTING GRAVENEY

Printed by P. Simonau.

G C–S

WALTON *upon Hill* **CHURCH.** *N. W.*

Ground Plan

Scale of   50   100 Feet

136.   **WALTON-ON-THE-HILL**

WALTON upon Thames CHURCH. S.E.

Ground Plan.

Scale of   100 feet

137. WALTON ON THAMES

C.Burton del.

Printed by P.Simonau

WANDSWORTH CHURCH . S-W .

Ground Plan

Scale of

138. WANDSWORTH

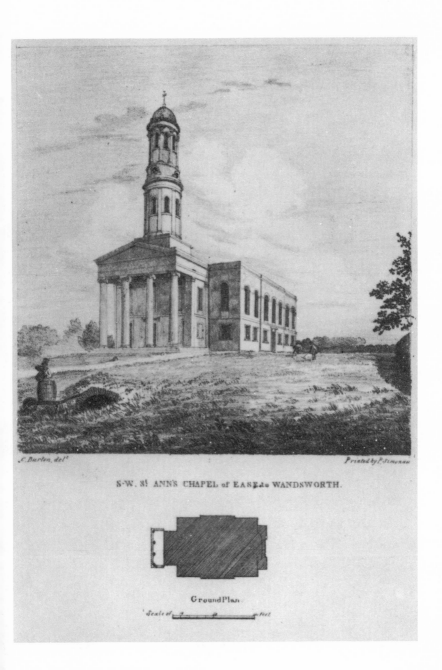

S.W. S! ANN'S CHAPEL of EASE to WANDSWORTH.

GroundPlan.

Scale of feet.

139.   WANDSWORTH, ST. ANNE

WARLINGHAM CHURCH. S E

Ground Plan

Scale of 0   50   100 Feet

140. WARLINGHAM

WEST CLANDON CHURCH East.

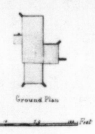

Ground Plan

Scale of _____ Feet

141. WEST CLANDON

WEST HORSLEY CHURCH *s.w.*

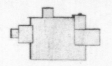

Ground Plan

142. WEST HORSLEY

WEST MOULSEY CHURCH &c.

Ground Plan

Scale of ⸻ Feet

143. WEST MOLESEY

WEYBRIDGE CHURCH. VK

Ground Plan.

Scale of [Feet]

144. WEYBRIDGE

C. Burton del.t   Printed by P. Simonau

WIMBLEDON CHURCH , S-W.

Ground Plan.

Scale   50   100 feet

145. WIMBLEDON

WINDLESHAM CHURCH. S.W.

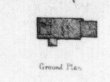

Ground Plan

Scale of .... Feet

146.   WINDLESHAM

BAGSHOT CHAPEL. N.E.

Ground Plan.

Scale of ... Feet

147. WINDLESHAM, BAGSHOT CHAPEL

BAGSHOT CHAPEL. *N,E.*

Ground Plan

Scale of ² ⁴ ²⁰ *Feet*

148.   WINDLESHAM, BAGSHOT CHAPEL

WISLEY CHURCH. N.W.

Ground Plan

Scale of   Feet.

149. WISLEY

C.Burton, del.   Printed by P.Simonau.

WITLEY CHURCH, S.E.

Ground Plan.

Scale of   20 feet

150. WITLEY

WOKING CHURCH. S.E

Ground
Plan

151. WOKING

WOLDINGHAM CHURCH. S.E.

Ground Plan

152. WOLDINGHAM

WONERSH CHURCH. N.W.

Ground Plan

Scale of   6,0   120 Feet.

153. WONERSH

WOODMANSTERNE, CHURCH, N.E.

Ground Plan

Scale of ⏐ 10 ⏐ 5 0 ⏐ 50 ⏐ Feet

154. WOODMANSTERNE

WORPLESDON CHURCH. S.W.

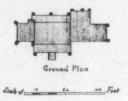

Ground Plan

Scale of 10 50 100 Feet

155. WORPLESDON

WOTTON CHURCH. S,E

Printed by P. Simonau.

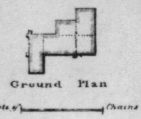

Ground Plan

Scale of |——————| Chains

156. WOTTON